# Conversational AI Revolution

# How Chatbots and Virtual Assistants Are Transforming Communication

Taylor Royce

# DEDICATION

To the visionaries, researchers, and pioneers influencing artificial intelligence's direction.

To the industrious brains that are constantly expanding the possibilities for human-machine cooperation and making sure that technology complements rather than replaces our collective wisdom.

To those who think AI should be developed responsibly and ethically, striking a balance between automation and human ingenuity, efficiency and empathy, and progress and humanity.

And to the generations to come, who will go on this adventure and change the way we connect, communicate, and create.

You should read this book.

# DISCLAIMER

This book is meant solely for educational and informational purposes. The author and publisher make no explicit or implicit guarantees or assurances about the content's correctness, application, fitness for a specific purpose, or completeness, even though every effort has been made to assure its accuracy, completeness, and dependability. As conversational AI research and technology continue to advance, the content in this book could change.

## No Legal or Professional Advice

This book's information should not be interpreted as technical, financial, legal, or professional advice. Before making any technological, legal, or business decisions based on the information provided, readers are urged to seek advice from knowledgeable experts. Any direct, indirect, incidental, or consequential damages resulting from the use or reliance on the information in this book are not the responsibility of the author or publisher.

## Disclaimer on AI Technology

Although this book examines current technology,

approaches, and trends in the quickly developing field of conversational AI, its information may become out of date as new advancements are made. Chatbots and virtual assistants are examples of AI systems that need to be used responsibly and in accordance with ethical standards and industry rules. Any misuse, bias, or unforeseen effects resulting from the usage of AI are not the author's responsibility.

## Third-Party Citations

Third-party tools, platforms, or technologies may be mentioned in this book. Such references are provided solely for informative purposes and do not imply sponsorship, endorsement, or association with any particular business, group, or item. Third-party brand names, trademarks, and intellectual property rights belong to their respective owners.

## Aspects of Regulation and Compliance

Readers should be aware that a number of legal and regulatory frameworks, including those pertaining to data privacy, such as the California Consumer Privacy Act (CCPA), the General Data Protection Regulation (GDPR), and other jurisdiction-specific restrictions, apply to conversational AI. The reader, company, or other entity using AI technologies is in charge of adhering to these rules. For specific regulatory problems, readers are recommended to seek expert legal counsel as this book does not offer legal compliance information.

## No Results Guaranteed

The approaches, tactics, and best practices covered in this book do not promise any certain outcome. Data quality, model training, business goals, and user interaction design are just a few of the variables that affect how well Conversational AI systems work. Both the publisher and the author disclaim any responsibility for the results that may arise from using the ideas in this book.

## Rights to Intellectual Property

The publisher and author of this book retain all rights to the text, structure, and formatting of this work. It is completely forbidden to reproduce, distribute, or modify this content without prior written consent.

You agree to the terms of this disclaimer by reading this

book.

# CONTENTS

# ACKNOWLEDGMENTS

Without the help, direction, and encouragement of numerous people and organizations, the writing of this book would not have been feasible. I would like to take this time to sincerely thank everyone who helped create this work, whether directly or indirectly.

I want to start by sincerely thanking my family and close friends, who have been my biggest source of inspiration due to their everlasting support and belief in me. Throughout this process, your understanding, support, and patience have been invaluable to me.

I also want to express my sincere gratitude to the Conversational AI researchers, technologists, and thought leaders whose work made the insights presented in this book possible. The information offered here has been greatly influenced by the contributions of the AI community, both in academia and industry.

I want to express my gratitude to my mentors and colleagues for their advice, thought-provoking conversations, and helpful criticism. Your insights and knowledge have enhanced this book's content and solidified its framework.

We would especially like to thank the technical reviewers and editors who carefully examined the article to make sure it was accurate, coherent, and clear. Your meticulousness and commitment to quality have substantially raised the caliber of this book.

I also want to thank all of the developers, data scientists, and AI professionals around the world whose creativity and problem-solving propel Conversational AI forward. Your efforts keep pushing the limits of what AI is capable of and inspiring others.

Finally, I want to thank all of my readers for joining me on this trip, whether you are an AI enthusiast, researcher, developer, or someone who is interested in the future of AI. I sincerely hope that this book will provide you insightful knowledge and motivation to research, develop, and create in the field of conversational artificial intelligence.

Many thanks to all of you.

# CHAPTER 1

## AN OVERVIEW OF CONVERSATIONAL AI

One of the most revolutionary developments in the digital world is conversational AI, which allows robots to communicate with people in a natural, intuitive, and intelligent way. Understanding the foundations of conversational AI is becoming more and more crucial as businesses from a variety of industries implement AI-powered communication platforms. This chapter offers a thorough examination of conversational artificial intelligence (AI), including its definition, historical development, industry relevance, and the main technologies advancing it.

## 1.1 What is Conversational AI?

Artificial intelligence systems that can have conversations like a person are known as conversational AI. To enable smooth communication between humans and machines, these systems combine natural language processing (NLP), machine learning (ML), speech recognition, and contextual awareness. Conversational AI has the ability to understand, process, and produce human language dynamically, which makes interactions more intelligent and fluid than typical chatbots that rely on predefined responses.

Fundamentally, conversational AI seeks to close the gap between people and machines by facilitating meaningful, real-time interactions. A variety of media, such as text, voice, and even multimodal interfaces that blend spoken and visual components, can be used for these exchanges.

**Key Features of Conversational AI**

- Context Awareness: The capacity to recall previous exchanges and keep discussions on track.
- Adaptive Learning: Based on user behavior, this technique uses machine learning models to gradually enhance responses.
- Multimodal Communication: Facilitates communication through speech, text, and even graphic interfaces.
- Responses are more pertinent when the user's intent is recognized, which goes beyond keyword

matching.

- Personalization: Modifies answers according to user behavior, history, and preferences.

Numerous applications, such as chatbots, virtual assistants (like Siri and Alexa), customer care bots, and AI-driven communication tools, are powered by conversational AI. These solutions are improving consumer experiences, productivity, and efficiency in addition to completely changing how people use technology.

## 1.2 Conversational Systems' Development

Over the past few decades, there have been substantial changes in the development of conversational AI. Contextualizing this growth helps explain how contemporary AI-driven dialogue systems have developed to their current level of sophistication.

### First Chatbots Based on Rules

The early chatbots used basic rule-based pattern matching, including ELIZA (1966). These algorithms could only identify particular keywords and were dependent on predefined scripts. Although remarkable at the time, their inability to comprehend meaning made conversations tedious and mechanical.

## Statistical NLP's Ascent (1990s–Early 2000s)

Chatbots got increasingly complex as natural language processing (NLP) and machine learning advanced. statistical models were developed during this time to enhance language comprehension and enable AI to analyze text more efficiently.

## Deep Learning and Neural Networks (2010s - Present)

Conversational AI was transformed with the advent of deep learning, recurrent neural networks (RNNs), transformers, and large-scale language models. Machines can now understand context, provide human-like replies, and even forecast user intent with high accuracy thanks to technologies like GPT (Generative Pre-trained Transformer), BERT (Bidirectional Encoder Representations from Transformers), and T5 (Text-to-Text Transfer Transformer).

## The 2020s and Beyond: The Age of Generative AI

Conversational AI can now have real-time, dynamic discussions that feel natural and intuitive thanks to the development of ChatGPT, Bard, and multimodal AI systems. As they develop further, these AI systems are pushing the limits of proactive involvement, customisation, and contextual comprehension.

## 1.3 Relevance and Uses in Various Industries

More than merely a technical development, conversational AI has significant industry-wide ramifications that are changing how companies run and how consumers engage with digital services.

## 1. Improving Engagement and Customer Support

The automation of customer service is one of the most important uses of conversational AI. Chatbots driven by AI are able to:

- Manage large volumes of inquiries without the need for human assistance.
- Reduce wait times and increase customer satisfaction by offering instant responses.
- Provide 24/7 availability so that users can get help

whenever they need it.

- Examine consumer sentiment to tailor answers.

## 2. Transforming the Medical Field

Conversational AI is utilized in the healthcare sector for the following purposes:

- Virtual health assistants that assist patients with scheduling appointments, reminding them to take their medications, and providing symptom-checking services.
- AI-driven chatbots for mental health assistance, offering prompt advice for emotional stability and stress reduction.
- Healthcare triage systems that use AI analysis to evaluate symptoms and suggest medical interventions.

## 3. Revolutionizing Retail and E-Commerce

Conversational AI improves the online buying experience by:

- Based on user activity, offering individualized product recommendations.
- Using voice and text interactions to help customers

locate products.

- Refunds, order tracking, and post-purchase questions are all handled with ease.

## 4. Promoting Innovation in Banking and Finance

AI-driven chatbots and virtual assistants in the financial industry:

- Automate account management activities, like reviewing transaction history and balances.
- Help with security verification and fraud detection.
- Based on the user's spending patterns, provide individualized financial advice.

## 5. Increasing Business Productivity

Enterprise apps are using conversational AI more and more to:

- Automate repetitive processes like reminders and meeting scheduling.
- Enhance teamwork with virtual assistants driven by AI.
- Offer data-driven decision support and real-time insights.

# 1.4 The main technologies that underpin conversational artificial intelligence

In order to build intelligent and responsive communication systems, conversational AI depends on a number of essential technologies.

## 1. Natural Language Processing (NLP)

NLP makes it possible for computers to comprehend and process human language. It includes:

- Tokenization is the process of dividing text into smaller parts for analysis.
- Finding important entities, such as names, dates, and locations, is known as Named Entity Recognition (NER).
- Recognizing the emotional tone of a communication is known as sentiment analysis.

## 2. Deep Learning and Machine Learning

Conversational AI is capable of learning from enormous volumes of data thanks to machine learning models, particularly deep learning frameworks.

- Identifying intricate patterns in human speech is one

of the tasks that neural networks assist with.

- Accurately predicting user intent.
- Enhancing the flow of conversations through ongoing education.

## 3. Text-to-Speech (TTS) and Speech Recognition

Voice-based Conversational AI applications depend on:

- The process of turning spoken words into text for processing is known as Automatic Speech Recognition (ASR).
- Text-to-voice (TTS) Engines: Transform text responses into voice that sounds natural.

## 4. Knowledge Graphs and Context Management

Contextual AI systems store and retrieve structured data using knowledge graphs. This facilitates the provision of true, fact-based answers.

- Comprehending the usage query context over time.
- Improving user experience and personalization.

## 5. Large Language Models (LLMs) and Generative AI

New developments in generative AI and transformer-based models (such as GPT-4) have greatly enhanced

Conversational AI's capacity to: - Produce text responses that are logical and human-like.

- Comprehend complex user inquiries.
- Modify answers according to previous conversations.

Conversational AI is quickly changing how people and machines communicate, allowing for more intelligent and natural communication. A full overview of conversational AI was given in this chapter, covering everything from its concept and historical development to its real-world applications and underlying technology. Conversational AI will become even more multimodal, personalized, and context-aware as AI develops, opening the door to smarter interactions across all digital platforms.

The foundation of conversational AI, Natural Language Processing (NLP), will be covered in further detail in the upcoming chapter, which will examine how machines comprehend and interpret human language.

# CHAPTER 2

## AN OVERVIEW OF CONVERSATIONAL AI'S NATURAL LANGUAGE PROCESSING (NLP)

The foundation of conversational AI is natural language processing (NLP), which gives computers the ability to comprehend, interpret, and produce human language. This chapter explores the foundations of natural language processing (NLP), its primary methods, the difficulties it encounters in conversational AI, and emerging trends that are influencing the field.

## 2.1 How Does NLP Operate and What Is It?

The goal of the artificial intelligence (AI) discipline of natural language processing (NLP) is to enable robots to comprehend and react to human language in a meaningful and contextually relevant manner. It processes and analyzes speech and text by combining deep learning, machine learning, and computational linguistics methods.

Fundamentally, NLP analyzes the structure of language, breaks it down into smaller parts, and uses context to infer meaning. There are two main groups into which this technique falls:

- Natural Language Understanding (NLU): This entails determining entities, intent, sentiment, and context in order to derive meaning from speech or text.
- NLG stands for Natural Language Generation. In order to enable AI-driven responses that resemble human communication, this focuses on creating text or speech that sounds human.

**NLP uses several levels of linguistic analysis, such as:**

- Lexical analysis is the study of words and their definitions.
- Syntactic Analysis: Examining grammar and sentence construction.
- Semantic Analysis: Contextual understanding of meaning.

- Using conversational details to determine the intended meaning is known as pragmatic analysis.

Together, these procedures enable conversational AI systems to comprehend user inquiries, retrieve pertinent data, and produce responses that meet human standards.

## 2.2 Sentiment analysis, Named Entity Recognition (NER), and tokenization

NLP uses a number of essential methods to analyze and comprehend text. Tokenization, named entity recognition (NER), and sentiment analysis are a few of the most crucial ones.

### Tokenization

The technique of tokenization involves dividing a text into smaller parts called tokens, which can be words or sentences. This facilitates the organization of unstructured text data for subsequent processing.

- Word tokenization is the process of breaking a

statement up into its component words.

- The process of dividing text into sentences for analysis is known as sentence tokenization.
- Subword tokenization is the process of breaking words down into more manageable chunks, which is helpful for languages with intricate morphology.

By handling each token as a separate processing unit, tokenization helps AI models interpret language more efficiently.

## Recognition of Named Entities (NER)

One of the most important NLP tasks is Named Entity Recognition (NER), which recognizes and categorizes named entities in text, including names of individuals, groups, places, dates, and numbers. For conversational AI to extract pertinent information from user questions, this is crucial.

**Named entity categories include, for example:**

- People: Recognizing names (like "Elon Musk").

- Organizations: Identifying business names, such as "Tesla, Inc."
- places: Taking geographic places (like "New York") and extracting them.
- Time and Dates: Comprehending time expressions, such as "March 10, 2025"

Chatbots and virtual assistants can utilize NER to glean specific information from user inquiries and deliver more pertinent answers.

## Analysis of Sentiment

Text's emotional tone can be ascertained through sentiment analysis. It enables conversational AI to comprehend user sentiment and react accordingly.

- "I love this product!" is an example of a positive sentiment, when the user expresses enjoyment or contentment.
- Negative Sentiment: The user expresses dissatisfaction or unhappiness, such as "This is terrible service."

- The user does not convey a strong sense of enthusiasm or negative, as evidenced by the phrase "I need help with my order."

Conversational AI can improve customer experience and engagement by adjusting its responses according to the user's emotional state by integrating sentiment analysis.

## 2.3 NLP Difficulties for Conversational AI

Even while NLP has advanced significantly, there are still a number of obstacles to overcome before it can be applied to conversational AI. These difficulties include ethical issues, ambiguity, and sophisticated language.

## Recognizing Ambiguity and Context

Words and phrases in human language can have several meanings depending on the situation, making it frequently confusing. For example, the term "bank" can describe either the side of a river or a financial organization. To address such misunderstandings, conversational AI systems need sophisticated context-aware models.

## Managing Code-Switched and Multilingual Languages

Many users flip between languages or converse in many languages at once (code-switching). Conversational AI needs to be able to digest information in multiple languages while comprehending and producing responses accurately.

## Idiomatic Expressions and Sarcasm

An important problem for NLP is identifying irony, idioms, and sarcasm. "Oh great, another error!" is an example of a sentence that appears positive but is actually negative. To identify these language subtleties, AI models need to be trained on a variety of datasets using complex techniques.

## Language Model Bias

Large datasets, which may contain biases found in human language, are used to train AI algorithms. NLP models have the potential to provide biased replies depending on political beliefs, gender, or race if left unchecked. To lessen these problems, developers must use strategies like bias detection and fairness optimization.

## Processing in Real Time and Latency

Real-time response generation and query processing are essential for conversational AI. However, latency problems might arise due to the computational cost of NLP models, particularly large-scale deep learning models. To improve performance, cloud-based processing and effective model tuning are required.

## 2.4 Upcoming Developments in NLP

NLP is always changing due to developments in computational linguistics, deep learning, and machine learning. The future of natural language processing in conversational AI is being shaped by a number of new phenomena.

## Large Language Models (LLMs) and Transformer-Based Models

NLP has been transformed by the emergence of transformer-based models, such Google's BERT and OpenAI's GPT series. These models make use of deep learning to improve language comprehension, paving the way for extremely complex conversational AI.

## Zero-Shot and Few-Shot Education

For training, traditional NLP models need a lot of labeled data. By enabling models to complete tasks with little to no previous training data, few-shot and zero-shot learning help AI systems become more adaptive to novel challenges.

## Emotionally Intelligent and Context-Aware AI

Conversational AI systems in the future will get better at comprehending user preferences, emotions, and long-term context. AI-driven communications will become more human-like as a result of improved tailored connections.

## Using Multimodal AI Integration

NLP's future lies in combining it with other AI modalities, such speech recognition and computer vision, to provide more engaging and dynamic dialogues. For more complex interactions, virtual assistants will be able to process text, voice, and images all at once.

**Ethical AI and Reducing Bias**

Addressing biases and ethical issues will be a primary focus as NLP develops. To ensure ethical AI use, researchers are concentrating on creating more equitable and transparent AI models.

The foundation of conversational AI is Natural Language Processing (NLP), which gives computers the ability to comprehend, process, and produce human language. NLP still has issues with bias, ambiguity, and real-time processing despite its progress. But as AI develops quickly, natural language processing (NLP) is set to advance, opening the door for conversational AI systems that are smarter, more ethical, and sensitive to context. Businesses and developers may create more efficient AI-driven conversational interfaces that revolutionize human-machine interaction by comprehending the foundations and difficulties of natural language processing.

# CHAPTER 3

## CONVERSATIONAL AI SYSTEM ARCHITECTURE

The ability of conversational AI systems to comprehend, process, and react to natural language inputs has completely changed human-computer interaction. These systems have a complicated architecture with many interconnected parts that cooperate to enable smooth communication. The basic elements of a conversational AI system are examined in this chapter, along with the significance of dialogue management and context retention, the function of knowledge bases and database integration, and the differences between rule-based and machine learning-driven AI.

## 3.1 Conversational AI System Components

Each of the many interconnected parts that make up a well-designed conversational AI system is in charge of managing a distinct facet of interaction. These elements guarantee that the AI can effectively absorb inputs, produce insightful answers, and continuously pick up new skills via user interactions.

## 1. The engine for natural language processing (NLP)

A conversational AI system's NLP engine is its fundamental component. It makes it possible for machines to understand and produce human language. The components of the NLP engine are:

- Natural Language Understanding (NLU) recognizes purpose, entities, and context to derive meaning from user input.
- Based on processed inputs, Natural Language Generation (NLG) generates responses that resemble those of a human.

## 2. Text-to-Speech (TTS) Processing and Speech Recognition

- Automatic Speech Recognition (ASR): Transforms spoken language into text so the AI can execute voice commands.
- Voice-based interactions are made possible via the

conversion of text-based responses into spoken language, or text-to-speech (TTS).

## 3. The system for managing dialogue

- Maintaining context and deciding on the next response based on past exchanges allows one to orchestrate discussions.
- It guarantees logical and seamless transitions between various subjects or goals.

## 4. AI Algorithms and Machine Learning Models

- Modern conversational AI systems are powered by neural networks, deep learning models, and reinforcement learning strategies.
- By learning from enormous chat datasets, these models enable AI to get better over time.

## 5. Integration of Knowledge Bases and Databases

- Accurate replies are provided by storing both structured and unstructured information.
- When creating responses, the AI may now access historical interactions, facts, and contextual information.

**6. The sixth layer is called User Interface (UI) and Experience (UX).**

- Specifies how the conversational AI system is used by users.
- It could be a voice assistant, chatbot, or multimodal system that combines voice, text, and images.

**7. Third-Party Integrations and APIs**

- Enables the AI to establish connections with databases, enterprise systems, and external apps.
- Assures smooth communication between AI and business tools such as e-commerce platforms, payment gateways, and customer relationship management (CRM) software.

Together, these elements guarantee that conversational AI systems can deliver precise, pertinent, and captivating user interactions.

**3.2 Context Retention and Dialogue Management**

The capacity to control discussion and preserve context is

one of the hallmarks of a successful conversational AI system. Modern AI systems must remain coherent throughout discussions, in contrast to older chatbots that react in discrete steps.

**Dialogue Management Is Important**

Making sure that discussions have a logical flow is the responsibility of dialogue management. It enables AI systems to:

- Monitor the conversation's progress and keep it on track.
- Respond to disruptions and naturally carry on conversations.
- Oversee several threads of conversations at once.

**Techniques for Context Retention**

AI systems employ a variety of techniques to maintain context during several conversations.

**1. Session-Based Context Retention:**
- Keeps track of the user's requests while the session is active.

- When context does not need to last beyond the talk, it is useful for brief exchanges.

## 2. Long-Term Memory and Persistent Context:

- Enables AI to retain previous exchanges for longer than a single session.
- Recalling past preferences and information improves customisation.

## 3. Intent and Slot-Filling Techniques:

- Recognizes the information that is lacking from a user's inquiry and requests explanation.
- For instance, if a user inputs, "Book a flight," the AI can inquire, "Where are you going?"

## 4. Dialogue Trees and Reinforcement Learning Approaches:

- Dialogue trees guarantee logical interactions by defining structured conversational paths.
- AI reactions based on feedback loops are enhanced by reinforcement learning models.

AI-driven discussions feel natural, human-like, and

responsive to user demands when dialogue management is done well.

## 3.3 Knowledge Bases and Database Integration

For conversational AI systems to produce precise and insightful responses, they frequently need access to enormous volumes of data. Integration with databases and knowledge bases is required for this.

### Knowledge Base Types

**1. Static Knowledge Bases:**
- Include pre-established information, including firm policies and frequently asked questions.
- Self-service portals and customer support bots use it.

**2. Secondly, dynamic knowledge bases:**
- Updated frequently with fresh data derived from user interactions.
- Found in adaptive learning platforms and recommendation systems driven by AI.

## 3. there are two types of knowledge bases:

- structured and unstructured. Structured databases store data in relational tables with pre-established schemas.
- These repositories of unstructured data may include emails, papers, or articles that are subjected to NLP analysis by AI algorithms.

## Incorporating Databases into Conversational AI

For AI systems to retrieve real-time information, they need to communicate with external databases. This comprises:

- Customer Support Bots: retrieving user settings, troubleshooting manuals, and previous orders.
- Virtual Assistants: Having access to cloud-based storage, calendars, and emails.
- E-commerce AI: Updating order statuses, processing payments, and checking inventories.

## Knowledge Retrieval APIs

Conversational AI frequently works with APIs to dynamically retrieve pertinent data. Among the examples are:

- The Google Knowledge Graph API gives AI access to factual information from online sources.
- CRM Integration (HubSpot, Salesforce): Obtains customer histories and profiles.
- AI-powered assistants can better handle commercial procedures like supply chain tracking with the aid of enterprise resource planning (ERP) systems.

AI systems can provide more intelligent and contextually relevant replies by utilizing well-structured knowledge bases and interacting with databases.

## 3.4 Rule-Based AI vs. Machine Learning

Both machine learning (ML) techniques and conventional rule-based approaches can be used to create conversational AI systems. Each has unique benefits and drawbacks.

### AI Based on Rules

Decision trees and prewritten scripts are the foundation of rule-based AI. It generates answers using if-then logic that has been manually programmed.

## Benefits:

- Extremely controllable and predictable.
- Perfect for straightforward interactions, like those of FAQ bots.
- It uses very little computer power.

## Restrictions:

- Unexpected or complicated queries cannot be handled.
- Lacks flexibility and contextual awareness.
- To increase functionality, manual updates are necessary.

## AI Based on Machine Learning

AI systems can learn from data and get better over time thanks to machine learning models, particularly deep learning-based techniques.

- The ability to comprehend unstructured material and derive meaning from context is one of its advantages.

- Gains knowledge from user interactions and becomes better with time.
- Personalized suggestions, intent recognition, and sentiment analysis are supported.

- It requires a lot of training data, which is one of its limitations.
- Biases depending on training datasets are likely to exist.
- computationally costly and necessitates a strong infrastructure.

## Hybrid AI Methods

Many conversational AI systems use a hybrid model in order to get beyond the drawbacks of both rule-based and machine learning techniques. This includes:

- Employing frameworks based on rules to facilitate organized interactions.
- Applying machine learning to intricate, context-specific queries.

- Refining AI-generated responses by combining human-in-the-loop techniques.

The intricacy of the use case, the data at hand, and the requirement for flexibility all influence the decision between rule-based AI and machine learning-driven AI.

A combination of natural language processing (NLP), dialogue management, database integration, and AI-driven decision-making is the foundation of conversational AI systems. In order to provide interactions that are human-like, effective systems incorporate machine learning models, intelligently manage context, and draw on both organized and unstructured knowledge sources. Developers can create dependable, scalable, and context-aware conversational AI systems that improve user experiences in a variety of sectors by comprehending these elements and how they interact.

# CHAPTER 4

## COMPREHENDING THE DISTINCTIONS BETWEEN CHATBOTS AND VIRTUAL ASSISTANTS

The phrases chatbots and virtual assistants are frequently used interchangeably as artificial intelligence (AI) develops. These two technologies, however, have different functions and differ in their degrees of complexity. Although the goal of both is to make human-machine interactions easier, there are substantial differences in their capabilities, underlying technologies, and use cases.

The basic distinctions between chatbots and virtual assistants are examined in this chapter, along with their unique features, a comparison of their advantages and disadvantages, and the direction these technologies will go in the future.

### 4.1 Describe chatbots.

Chatbots are artificial intelligence (AI)-powered applications created to mimic user chats. Their primary purpose is to help with question answering, response automation, and the provision of predetermined information through text-based or voice-enabled interfaces.

## Key Features of Chatbots

- AI-Powered or Rule-Based: While some chatbots follow preset scripts, others use machine learning (ML) and natural language processing (NLP) to understand user inquiries.
- Restricted Functionality and Scope: Typically, chatbots manage standardized tasks like scheduling appointments, responding to frequently asked questions, and handling straightforward transactions.
- Interactions Based on Triggers: The majority of chatbots function inside preset conversation flows, which means that they react in response to preset triggers or phrases.
- Implementation Specific to Industry: Chatbots are frequently employed to effectively address regular questions in customer service, e-commerce, banking,

and healthcare.

## Chatbot Types

### 1. Rule-Based Chatbots:

- These chatbots use pre-established answer flows and decision trees to function.
- Limited ability to respond to unexpected or complicated consumer inquiries.
- It's regularly used in customer service to give prompt responses to commonly requested inquiries.

### 2. AI-Powered Chatbots:

- Make use of ML and NLP to comprehend and process user input in real-time.
- Capable of improving replies over time by learning from previous interactions.
- When a more organic exchange is needed, conversational interfaces are utilized.

### 3. Hybrid Chatbots:

- Integrate AI-driven capabilities with rule-based reasoning.

- Able to manage dynamic searches and structured interactions with context awareness.
- found in complex customer service systems that require both automated and human-like replies.

## 4.2 Virtual Assistants: What Are They?

More sophisticated AI systems known as virtual assistants are made to do a variety of activities beyond simple communication. These assistants communicate with people more intelligently and individually by using speech recognition, AI, and natural language processing.

## Virtual Assistants' Essential Features

- Context-Aware and Adaptive: Virtual assistants, in contrast to conventional chatbots, remember context during several conversations and tailor their responses according to user preferences.
- They can do a wide range of functions, including sending emails, controlling smart devices, getting real-time information, and creating reminders.
- Hands-free engagement is made possible by the fact

that many virtual assistants, including Google Assistant, Apple Siri, and Amazon Alexa, respond to voice instructions.

- The process of integrating third-party services: Applications, databases, and external APIs are connected to by virtual assistants in order to carry out tasks like scheduling, flight booking, and IoT device control.

## Virtual Assistant Types

**1.** Personal virtual assistants are designed to help individuals handle daily chores like searches and reminders.

- Examples include Alexa, Google Assistant, and Siri.

**2. Enterprise Virtual Assistants:** Enterprise virtual assistants are used in business settings to manage customer interactions, plan meetings, and automate procedures.

- Examples include Microsoft Cortana for business use and IBM Watson Assistant.

**3.** Task-specific virtual assistants are made for certain purposes, such technical support, healthcare support, or financial management.

- Examples include Ada (a healthcare AI assistant) and Erica (Bank of America).

## 4.3 Chatbot vs Virtual Assistant Comparison: Potential and Drawbacks

Despite their similarities, chatbots and virtual assistants differ when compared in terms of their use cases, processing power, and functionality.

**1.** Functionality Scope Chatbots are made for basic, task-specific interactions, including making appointments or answering frequently asked questions.

- Virtual assistants handle a variety of frequently complicated activities, including scheduling, automating tasks, and controlling smart devices.

## 2. Intelligence and Context Retention

- Chatbots don't have long-term memory and mostly answer instantaneous questions.
- Over time, virtual assistants increase response

accuracy, learn from interactions, and remember user preferences.

## 3. Integration Capabilities

- Chatbots usually connect to a business's own knowledge base or customer service system.
- A variety of external services, such as cloud storage, smart home appliances, and third-party APIs, are connected to virtual assistants.

## 4. Interaction Mode

- Chatbots mostly use text-based user interfaces, with voice support available on occasion.
- Virtual assistants combine voice and text-based communication with sophisticated speech recognition.

## 5. Use Cases

**Chatbots:**

- Automation of customer service.
- Managing the FAQ.
- Order monitoring and e-commerce assistance.

**Virtual Assistants:**

- Automation of smart homes.
- Task management for enterprises.
- Tailored AI-powered suggestions.

## 6. Restrictions:

## Chatbots:

- Have trouble having unstructured conversations.
- The inability to manage several jobs beyond their designated scope.

## Virtual assistants:

- Demand a lot of processing power.
- Because of data collection, privacy issues may arise.

Businesses and users can decide if a chatbot or virtual assistant is suitable for their requirements by being aware of these distinctions.

## 4.4 Chatbots and Virtual Assistants' Future

Chatbots and virtual assistants are developing to become more intelligent, interactive, and context-aware as artificial intelligence (AI) advances. The way people interact with machines will change as these technologies advance.

## Important Developments in Conversational AI

1. Future chatbots and virtual assistants will be able to provide more complex and emotionally sophisticated responses because of advancements in natural language processing and conversational artificial intelligence.

- Real-time text and speech interactions will be improved by AI models such as GPT-4 and subsequent versions.

## 2. More Personalization

- AI assistants will provide highly customized experiences by utilizing user history, preferences, and behavioral data.

- Context-aware computers are able to recall past exchanges and modify their replies accordingly.

## 3. Seamless Multimodal Interactions

- To provide more engaging user experiences, chatbots and virtual assistants will integrate text, audio, and visual components.

- Real-world applications like augmented reality (AR)

integration for education and shopping will be improved by smart assistants.

## 4. Improved Security and Privacy Measures

- As AI becomes more pervasive in daily life, protecting user data will require improved encryption and privacy-focused AI.
- AI adoption will be influenced by open AI policies and adherence to international laws (such as the CCPA and GDPR).

## 5. Expanded Industry Applications

- To improve user experiences and automate processes, chatbots and virtual assistants will be used more and more in sectors including healthcare, finance, education, and retail.
- Conversational agents powered by AI will help with personalized learning, investment advisory, and telemedicine.

## 6. Internet of Things and Metaverse Integration

- Virtual assistants will be essential to the metaverse, allowing users to move across virtual worlds with voice commands.

- AI-powered assistants will improve home automation and office productivity by interacting with IoT devices more effectively.

Despite their apparent similarities, chatbots and virtual assistants differ in terms of intelligence, functionality, and flexibility. While chatbots are most effective at structured, predetermined tasks, virtual assistants provide a more complex, versatile, and context-aware approach.

Chatbots and virtual assistants will both develop further as AI technology advances, becoming essential tools for homes, workplaces, and daily digital interactions. To decide if a chatbot, virtual assistant, or a combination of the two is the best option for their purposes, organizations and developers must thoroughly assess their requirements.

# CHAPTER 5

## DEVELOPING A MODEL FOR CONVERSATIONAL AI

A game-changing technology, conversational AI allows machines to engage with people in meaningful and natural ways. It takes careful planning, knowledge of machine learning principles, and the ability to adjust the model for the best user experience to create a strong conversational AI model.

From choosing the best frameworks and training techniques to maximizing conversational flow and guaranteeing a smooth deployment, this chapter offers a thorough examination of the essential processes involved in developing a conversational AI system.

## 5.1 Selecting Appropriate Platforms and Frameworks

A crucial first step in developing a conversational AI system is choosing the appropriate frameworks and platforms. The AI model's complexity, deployment needs, scalability, and ease of integration with current technologies are some of the variables that influence the decision.

## Important Things to Look for When Choosing a Conversational AI Framework

- **Type of Conversational AI System:** Whether the system will be a sophisticated virtual assistant driven by AI or a basic rule-based chatbot.
- Requirements for Integration: Integration with enterprise software, messaging platforms, or Internet of Things devices is required.
- The framework's capacity to manage growing user interactions as the system expands is known as scalability.
- Customization: The degree to which proprietary data must be used to refine the AI model.

## Common Frameworks and Platforms for Conversational AI

## 1. Google Dialogflow

- An effective framework for creating virtual assistants and chatbots powered by AI.
- Facilitates text-based and voice communication.
- Integrates with Google Cloud, making it suitable for enterprise applications.

## 2. Microsoft Bot Framework

- Enables the development of intelligent chatbots using Azure AI services.
- Supports multi-platform deployment, including Microsoft Teams and Slack.
- Offers advanced NLP capabilities through Azure Cognitive Services.

## 3. IBM Watson Assistant

- Uses AI-powered natural language understanding (NLU) to create conversational agents.
- Provides contextual awareness for improved interactions.
- Offers industry-specific solutions for customer support and enterprise automation.

## 4. Rasa Open Source

- A self-hosted, highly customizable framework for building AI chatbots.
- Supports machine learning-based dialogue management.
- Suitable for organizations requiring data privacy and full control over AI training.

## 5. Amazon Lex

- Designed for constructing chatbots and voice assistants using AWS cloud services.
- Integrates smoothly with Amazon Alexa and other AWS services.
- Uses deep learning models for speech recognition and intent detection.

The choice of framework should fit with business goals, technical competence, and deployment preferences.

## 5.2 Training Models with Supervised and Reinforcement Learning

Once a framework is selected, the next step is training the

AI model. Effective training helps the AI system to grasp user intent, respond appropriately, and improve over time. Training approaches largely fall into two categories: supervised learning and reinforcement learning.

**Supervised Learning in Conversational AI**

Supervised learning includes training the AI model on labeled datasets where input (user queries) and output (correct responses) are preset. This method is frequently used for training chatbots and virtual assistants, assuring excellent accuracy in responses.

**Steps in Supervised Learning for Conversational AI**

**1. Data Collection**
- Gather conversation logs, customer service interactions, and FAQ databases.
- Use diverse datasets to train the model on multiple linguistic variations.

**2. Preprocessing the Data**
- Tokenization is the process of dividing sentences

into words to facilitate analysis.

- Eliminating popular words that don't contribute meaning is known as "stopword removal."

- Lemmatization is the process of standardizing responses by breaking words down into their most basic forms.

## 3. Model Training

- To train the model to identify user intents, use labeled datasets.

- Apply NLP techniques such as Named Entity Recognition (NER) and Part-of-Speech (POS) tagging.

## 4. Testing and Validation

- Validate the trained model using test datasets.

- Measure accuracy based on how well it predicts correct responses.

Customer service chatbots, FAQ bots, and other structured conversational AI applications benefit greatly from supervised learning.

## Conversational AI Reinforcement Learning

AI models can get better by using reinforcement learning (RL), which learns from user interactions. Instead of relying on predefined labels, RL allows the AI to experiment with responses and refine its approach based on rewards or penalties.

### Key Aspects of Reinforcement Learning in AI Models

- Exploration vs. Exploitation: The model explores new response strategies while leveraging existing knowledge.
- Reward Mechanism: Correct responses are rewarded, while incorrect ones receive penalties.
- Continuous Learning: The AI adapts to user behavior, refining its conversational abilities over time.

Reinforcement learning is ideal for complex virtual assistants that require adaptive learning, such as AI-powered customer engagement platforms and personalized recommendation systems.

## 5.3 Optimizing Conversational Flow and User Experience

A well-structured conversational AI model must go beyond basic query-response mechanics to provide a smooth, intuitive user experience. Optimizing conversational flow ensures that users feel engaged and receive meaningful responses.

### Principles of Effective Conversational Flow

### 1. Context Awareness
- Retain past interactions to offer relevant responses.
- Utilize AI models that are based on memory to monitor past conversations.

### 2. Handling Ambiguity
- When a question is not clear, provide prompts for clarification.
- Use fallback mechanisms to guide users when AI does not understand the intent.

## 3. Personalization

- Adapt responses based on user preferences and past behavior.
- Integrate AI with CRM systems to personalize customer interactions.

## 4. Multimodal Capabilities

- Support both text and voice inputs.
- Implement visual elements where applicable, such as chatbot UI enhancements.

## 5. Speed and Efficiency

- Minimize response delays using optimized backend processing.
- Reduce unnecessary steps in user interactions to enhance efficiency.

A conversational AI model that is optimized increases user engagement and decreases friction.

# 5.4 Conversational AI System Testing and Implementation

Before a conversational AI model is deployed, thorough testing is essential to ensure accuracy, reliability, and security.

## Testing Methodologies for Conversational AI

1. Unit Testing: Verify individual components, such as NLP processing and intent recognition.

2. User Acceptance Testing (UAT): Test conversational flow with users in real-world scenarios.

3. To guarantee scalability, evaluate performance under high interaction volumes using load testing.

4. The fourth step is security testing, which involves looking for flaws in authentication and data privacy.

## Guides for Deployment

1. Cloud Deployment: Host AI models on cloud platforms (AWS, Google Cloud, Azure) for scalability.

2. On-Premises Deployment: Suitable for organizations with strict data security requirements.

3. Hybrid Deployment: Combine cloud and on-premises solutions for optimized performance.

Once deployed, continuous monitoring and iterative improvements are necessary to enhance AI performance based on user feedback.

Building a conversational AI model requires a systematic approach, starting with selecting the right frameworks, training AI models using supervised and reinforcement learning, optimizing user interactions, and deploying a robust system. As AI continues to advance, the future of conversational AI will be driven by enhanced contextual understanding, improved personalization, and seamless human-like interactions. Businesses investing in these technologies must ensure continuous improvements to meet evolving user expectations and industry demands.

# CHAPTER 6

## CONVERSATIONAL AI's BIAS AND ETHICAL ISSUES

The ethical ramifications of conversational AI systems' development and application must be addressed as they become more and more integrated into daily interactions, powering chatbots for healthcare, virtual assistants, and customer service, among other applications. Conversational AI is more than just a technical advancement; it affects decision-making, changes human communication, and has the potential to increase biases and violate user privacy.

This chapter explores the ethical issues surrounding conversational AI, such as the difficulties posed by bias in AI training data, the ethical obligations of AI developers, the significance of data security and privacy, and the legal frameworks controlling AI applications.

## 6.1 Handling Prejudice in AI Training Information

When societal biases are reflected in training data, bias in AI models develops, producing unfair or discriminatory results. Any bias in the data, whether from historical discrimination, cultural stereotypes, or incomplete representation, may be incorporated into the AI's decision-making processes because conversational AI systems learn from pre-existing datasets.

### Conversational AI Bias Sources

### 1. Data Collection Bias

- AI models depend on sizable datasets, some of which may come from unrepresentative or biased samples.
- A chatbot may have trouble understanding non-Western dialects, idioms, and cultural quirks if it is trained primarily on English-language data from Western users.

### 2. Labeling Bias

- To assist AI models in learning intent recognition

and contextual understanding, human annotators label data.

- When classifying responses, annotators might unintentionally introduce their own biases.

## 3. Algorithmic Bias

- AI models may disproportionately favor particular groups as they optimize for accuracy using training data.
- If previous hiring trends favored men over women, a chatbot used for job recruitment that is trained on historical hiring data may favor male applicants.

## 4. Deployment Bias

- Biases may be strengthened by the way AI is applied and engages with users.
- A chatbot that learns from user interactions might adopt discriminatory language if exposed to biased inputs.

## Strategies to Mitigate Bias

- Diverse and Representative Training Data:

Incorporate data from multiple demographics, cultures, and linguistic backgrounds to ensure inclusivity.

- Actively seek marginalized voices to balance AI learning.

## Bias identification and Auditing

- Implement bias identification tools to investigate AI outputs for discriminatory trends.
- Conduct periodic audits to ensure fairness in AI decision-making.

## Human Oversight and Intervention

- Allow AI systems to be monitored and corrected by human moderators.
- Implement feedback loops where users can report biased responses for review.

## Fairness-Aware Algorithms

- Use fairness-aware machine learning techniques that adjust model predictions to reduce discriminatory tendencies.

Bias in conversational AI is an ongoing challenge, but proactive measures can help build fairer, more equitable systems.

## 6.2 Ethical Use of Conversational AI

Beyond technical bias, the ethical deployment of conversational AI raises fundamental moral questions. AI systems interact with people in personal, professional, and sensitive contexts, necessitating ethical design principles to prevent harm.

### Key Ethical Principles in Conversational AI

### 1. Transparency

- Users should be notified when they are interacting with AI rather than a human.
- Organizations should disclose how AI models are developed, what data they use, and the limitations of AI-generated replies.

### 2. Accountability

- Developers and organizations must accept

accountability for AI judgments, especially in high-stakes settings like healthcare, banking, or legal services.

- Clear protocols should be in place for rectifying AI mistakes and addressing grievances.

## 3. Autonomy and User Control

- Users ought to be able to modify, take control of, or stop interacting with AI.
- Users shouldn't be coerced by AI into making choices they wouldn't otherwise make.

## 4. Avoiding Deception

- Conversational AI shouldn't falsely mimic people.
- Ethical AI design avoids manipulative language and ensures that AI-driven responses align with factual accuracy.

## Case Studies of Ethical Concerns in AI

- Facebook's AI Chatbots (2017): AI models invented their own language that humans could not understand, prompting fears about AI control.

- Amazon's AI Hiring Tool (2018): The AI system was shown to be biased against female applicants due to historical hiring data.

- Google Duplex (2018): The AI replicated human speech so successfully that it generated discussions on whether AI interactions should always disclose their non-human origin.

As AI gets more advanced, ethical considerations must remain a priority in AI governance.

## 6.3 Protecting Data Security and Privacy

From delicate medical talks to customer service queries, conversational AI systems handle enormous volumes of personal data. Preserving user confidence and avoiding exploitation depend on protecting this data.

**Conversational AI Privacy Risks**

1. Unauthorized Data Collection: AI systems frequently gather user input to enhance their models, which raises questions about potential abuse and

surveillance.

2. Data Storage and Retention: Storing conversational logs can expose users to privacy breaches if security measures are inadequate.

3. Third-Party Data Sharing: Some AI providers share user interactions with advertisers or external vendors, creating potential for data exploitation.

## Optimal Methods for Protecting Data in Conversational AI

- End-to-end encryption: Protect user data from unwanted access by encrypting chats.

- User Consent Mechanisms: Prior to retaining or examining chat logs, receive express user consent. Permit users to request the deletion of their data.

- Minimization of Data Collection: Retain only the data required to support AI operations.

- To safeguard user identification, personal identifiers are removed from saved chat data using the processes of anonymization and pseudonymization.

## Security Measures for AI Systems

- Cloud Infrastructure and safe APIs: Make sure AI apps use safe APIs to stop data breaches.
- Regular Security Audits: To find vulnerabilities, perform regular security audits.
- Compliance with Cybersecurity Standards: Adhere to security frameworks like NIST cybersecurity recommendations and ISO/IEC 27001.

In addition to being required by law, conversational AI systems have a basic duty to protect user privacy and security.

## 6.4 Conversational AI Regulations and Compliance

The necessity of legal frameworks to control AI ethics, data privacy, and bias mitigation has been acknowledged by governments and regulatory agencies. Organizations deploying conversational AI must comply with global regulations to avoid legal consequences and build ethical AI systems.

## Key AI Regulations and Frameworks

## 1. Europe's General Data Protection Regulation (GDPR)

- Enforces stringent privacy and data protection regulations for users.
- Demands that AI firms give concise justifications for judgments made using AI.

## 2. The United States' California Consumer Privacy Act (CCPA)

- Users are given the right to know what personal information is gathered.
- Users can choose not to share their data with outside parties.

## 3. AI Act (Proposed by the European Union)

- Classifies AI systems based on risk levels and imposes harsher controls on high-risk AI applications.

## 4. ISO/IEC 42001 AI Management System Standard

- Provides recommendations for ethical AI development and risk management.

## 5. China's AI Regulations

- Demands that AI systems adhere to security protocols and ethical guidelines set forth by the government.

## Techniques for AI Developers to Comply with Regulations

- Legal Consultation: To guarantee compliance, collaborate with legal and AI ethics specialists.
- Transparency Reports: Issue reports detailing the data processing and storage practices of AI systems.
- User Education: Educate users on their rights concerning data privacy and AI interactions.

Organizations must proactively align AI systems with legal and ethical requirements because compliance is not optional due to changing regulatory landscapes.

Although conversational AI has many advantages, there are also serious ethical issues. Responsible AI development requires addressing bias, maintaining privacy, guaranteeing transparency, and adhering to legal requirements. The ethical stewardship of AI will determine whether it benefits humanity fairly or perpetuates social inequalities as it becomes more integrated into daily life. Organizations may build trust and establish systems that genuinely improve human communication by giving ethical AI development top priority.

# CHAPTER 7

## IMPROVING CONVERSATIONAL AI's USER EXPERIENCE

Conversational AI success is largely dependent on user experience (UX). Conversational AI systems must offer meaningful, effective, and natural interactions, in contrast to typical software applications where users choose from pre-established possibilities. Customer service, transactions, companionship, and even accessibility for those with impairments can all be enhanced by a well-designed AI assistant.

Personalization, multimodal interactions, error management, and continuous learning are some of the aspects of conversational AI that go into improving the user experience. Every one of these elements helps to build an AI system that is user-friendly, effective, and responsive to their demands. In addition to looking at best practices for maximizing user experience in AI-driven interactions, this chapter delves deeply into these essential components.

## 7.1 Context Awareness and Personalization

The capacity of a conversational AI system to customize interactions according to user preferences, past exchanges, and contextual data is known as personalization. The AI can better comprehend user intent, recall previous exchanges, and respond in a way that fits the current discussion thanks to context awareness.

### Personalization's Function in Conversational AI

By making interactions more meaningful and relevant, personalization increases user engagement. AI may adjust to each user's unique needs rather than providing generic answers, resulting in a smooth and delightful experience.

- AI assistants have the ability to provide recommendations for goods, services, or information based on a user's past interactions.
- By remembering consumer preferences, e-commerce chatbots can customize the buying experience.

- AI systems have the ability to remember previous conversations, which stops users from repeating themselves.

- For a more seamless user experience, virtual assistants can keep track of past questions, appointments, and reminders.

Conversational AI has the ability to modify its language style according to user preferences thanks to its Adaptive Language and Tone feature.

- While a professional tone might be preferred in business settings, a more informal tone might be appropriate for a younger audience.

## Context Awareness Implementation

Conversational AI can understand user intent by taking past interactions and outside variables into account thanks to context awareness.

Session-Based Context Retention: To guarantee continuity, AI should preserve the context of conversations within a session.

- For instance, the AI should recognize that "tomorrow" relates to the weather in New York if a user asks, "What's the weather like in New York?" and then adds, "What about tomorrow?"

Long-Term Context Awareness: Certain AI models maintain user preferences throughout several exchanges.

- For instance, a chatbot that specializes in personal finance might remember a user's spending patterns and offer customized financial guidance.

Multi-Turn Conversations: AI should be able to manage multiple turns well in order to handle complex dialogues.

- For instance, an AI travel assistant should be able to comprehend the following queries: "Find me a flight to London," followed by "Book a hotel near the city center."

Conversational AI may produce more meaningful and productive interactions by combining personalization with context awareness, which will increase user engagement and happiness.

## 7.2 Multimodal AI: Interactions via Voice, Text, and Vision

Multimodal systems that integrate text, audio, and visual components to improve communication have emerged as a result of AI's development. Multimodal AI enhances accessibility, enriches user interactions, and provides a more natural method for people to engage with AI-powered devices.

### Why Multimodal AI Matters

Traditional text-based chatbots are useful, but they have limits. Some users prefer speaking over typing, while others may benefit from visual components such as graphics, graphs, or videos. Multimodal AI enables for more dynamic interactions.

Enhanced User Engagement: Combining voice, text, and graphics makes interactions more intuitive.

- Example: A virtual shopping assistant that shows product photos while explaining their features by voice.

Accessibility Improvements: Multimodal AI enables people with disabilities to interact through their preferred manner.

- Example: A voice assistant that delivers text captions for hearing-impaired consumers.

## Key Components of Multimodal AI

### 1. Voice Recognition and Speech Synthesis

- AI can convert spoken words into text through speech-to-text (STT).
- Responses based on text can be transformed into spoken output using text-to-speech (TTS).

### 2. Text-Based Interactions

- Email, messaging apps, and chat interfaces are ways that users can interact with AI.
- For precise intent recognition, text-based AI should facilitate natural language understanding (NLU).

### 3. Visual Integration

- AI can support text and voice interactions by displaying interactive elements, videos, or charts.
- An example would be a chatbot that functions as a virtual doctor and offers medical advice in addition to anatomical illustrations.

## Difficulties with Multimodal AI Implementation

- Seamless Integration: AI systems need to be able to synchronize various communication channels with ease.
- Computational Complexity: Multimodal AI necessitates sophisticated machine learning models and increased processing power.
- Context Switching: AI ought to be able to switch between modes according to user preference without becoming confused.

Conversational AI becomes more adaptable and user-friendly by integrating multimodal capabilities, serving a wider range of users with different interaction preferences.

## 7.3 Managing Incorrect User Input and Errors

Conversational AI needs to be built with the ability to respond to unexpected user inputs and manage errors with grace. Misunderstood inquiries, unclear requests, or user error can all result in errors. Frustration and a lack of faith in AI systems might result from poor error handling.

### Typical Error Handling Difficulties

- Misinterpretation of User Intent: If a query is phrased in an uncommon or sophisticated way, AI may misunderstand it.
- Out-of-Scope Requests: Users may pose queries that are outside the scope of the AI's knowledge base.
- Ambiguous Inputs: When questions are unclear, AI may have trouble deducing meaning.
- It is expected that chatbots will be able to identify and fix typical typographical and spelling errors.

### Effective Strategies for Handling Errors

# 1. Clarification Prompts

- Instead of providing incorrect answers, AI should seek clarification.

- Example: If a user asks, "Book a table for Friday," the AI should respond, "What time would you like your reservation?"

# 2. Fallback Responses

- When AI cannot process a request, it should suggest an alternative.

- Example: "I'm sorry, I don't have that information. Would you like me to connect you with a human agent?"

# 3. Continuous Improvement and Error Logging

- AI should improve future encounters by learning from prior mistakes.

- Keeping an eye on user feedback enhances response precision.

# 4. Managing Harmful or Offensive Inputs

- AI should be protected from offensive or abusive language.

- Example: If a user inputs offensive content, the AI can answer with a neutral comment such, "I'm here to facilitate useful talks. Let's keep it respectful."

AI can offer a more streamlined and dependable user experience by putting these tactics into practice.

## 7.4 Ongoing Education and Development

Conversational AI ought to be built with the ability to change over time in response to user input, behavior, and new trends. AI can provide more accurate, efficient, and relevant interactions thanks to ongoing learning.

## Methods for AI Continuous Learning

1. Real-world user interactions should be used to refine AI models through Supervised Learning from User Feedback.
- AI can learn from mistakes and increase accuracy thanks to feedback mechanisms.

## 2. Unsupervised Learning for Pattern Recognition
- AI is able to examine user behavior to spot new

subjects or trends.

- This enables AI to foresee user requirements and take proactive measures.

## 3. Regular Model Updates and Retraining

- To avoid out-of-date replies, AI has to be updated with fresh data on a regular basis.
- For instance, a financial chatbot must be informed about the most recent developments in the stock market.

## 4. Training for Humans in the Loop (HITL)

- AI's learning process should be validated by human monitoring.
- A human assessment makes sure AI doesn't perpetuate prejudices or inaccurate answers.

Conversational AI maintains its adaptability and relevance through constant improvement, guaranteeing a top-notch user experience.

Personalization, multimodal capabilities, efficient error management, and ongoing learning are all needed to improve the user experience in conversational AI. AI developers can produce systems that are interesting, effective, and responsive to user requirements by concentrating on these areas. As AI develops, putting the user experience first will be essential to creating AI systems that genuinely improve human relationships.

# CHAPTER 8

## CONVERSATIONAL AI's PRACTICAL USES

Many industries have seen a shift thanks to conversational AI, which has also changed how people and organizations use technology. AI-driven conversational agents are revolutionizing efficiency, accessibility, and user engagement through anything from automating customer service to offering tailored financial advice and improving educational opportunities.

The practical uses of conversational AI in customer service, healthcare, finance, and education are examined in this chapter. The use of AI-powered chatbots, voice assistants, and intelligent virtual agents has resulted in notable advancements in each of these industries.

## 8.1 Conversational AI in E-commerce and Customer Service

In the past, handling questions, grievances, and service requests has required large teams of people and a lot of resources. Conversational AI has considerably increased efficiency in this industry by delivering 24/7 automated assistance, lowering wait times, and maintaining consistent service quality.

## AI's Advantages for Customer Service

- In contrast to human agents, AI-powcred assistants are available around-the-clock to offer assistance.
- Time zones don't have to stop businesses from serving clients throughout the world.

## Decreased Operational Costs

- By automating routine questions, huge support teams are not as necessary.
- AI systems respond to routine inquiries, freeing up human agents to work on more complicated problems.

## Improved Response Time

- AI chatbots cut down on wait times by immediately

retrieving information from knowledge sources.

- Consumers get instant access to troubleshooting instructions, order status updates, and solutions to frequently asked questions.

## Accuracy and Consistency

- AI makes sure that answers are precise and consistent throughout all exchanges.
- AI does not get tired or biased like human agents do.

## E-commerce AI

Conversational AI is used by e-commerce platforms to enhance client interaction and enhance purchasing experiences.

Personalized Shopping Assistance: AI chatbots make product recommendations based on customer preferences, browsing history, and previous purchases.

- As an illustration, an AI assistant makes fashion recommendations based on a customer's previous purchases and current styles.

Order Management and Tracking: AI-powered assistants allow customers to change purchases, check order statuses, and request refunds.

- For instance, real-time shipment and projected arrival time updates are provided via a chatbot.

Conversational Commerce: AI makes it possible for chat apps to conduct transactions smoothly.

- Consumers can stay in the chat window while conducting product searches, adding goods to their cart, and completing purchases.

Businesses may increase customer satisfaction, optimize processes, and boost revenues by implementing AI to improve customer care and e-commerce transactions.

## 8.2 AI in Healthcare: Symptom Checkers and Virtual Physicians

By increasing access to medical help and enhancing patient outcomes, conversational AI is revolutionizing the healthcare industry. AI-powered virtual assistants support medical practitioners with administrative duties, offer health advice, and detect ailments.

## Symptom Checkers and Virtual Health Assistants

Initial Diagnosis and Triage AI chatbots use medical databases to evaluate symptoms and recommend potential illnesses.

- For instance, when a user inputs symptoms, a chatbot can deliver a preliminary diagnosis and suggest whether or not to seek medical help.

Appointment Scheduling: AI assistants work with medical systems to schedule appointments with doctors.

- For instance, an AI-powered voice assistant that verifies a doctor's availability helps a patient make an appointment.

Health Monitoring and Medication Reminders: AI chatbots keep an eye on chronic illnesses and remind users to take their medications.

- For instance, diabetic patients are reminded to check their blood sugar levels via a virtual assistant.

## AI to Support Mental Health

Conversational Therapy Bots: AI-driven chatbots for mental health offer coping mechanisms and emotional support.

- For instance, Woebot and other AI applications help people with anxiety and depression by using cognitive behavioral therapy (CBT) techniques.

Crisis Management: AI systems are able to identify crisis signals and point users in the direction of emergency resources.

- For instance, a chatbot can identify suicide thoughts during a conversation and provide the numbers of crisis hotlines.

AI in healthcare improves patient access to medical information while also reducing administrative hassles and increasing efficiency for healthcare professionals.

## 8.3 AI in Finance: Intelligent Helpers for Investing and Banking

AI-powered assistants have been adopted by the finance sector to offer investment insights, financial planning, and individualized banking experiences. Conversational AI promotes productivity, security, and decision-making in banking and investment services.

### Banking AI

AI chatbots answer banking questions including balance checks, transaction histories, and loan applications as part of Automated Customer Service.

- For instance, a chatbot within a banking app helps consumers with bill payment and money transfers.

Fraud Detection and Security: AI detects transactions that seem suspicious and warns users of possible fraud.

- For instance, when a virtual assistant notices an odd transaction pattern, it asks the user to confirm that it is legitimate.

Voice-Activated financial: AI-powered voice assistants allow users to conduct financial activities using speech commands.

- Example: Using a smart speaker, a client requests that a virtual assistant check their account balance.

## AI in Wealth and Investment Management

Robo-Advisors for Investment Decisions: AI-driven investment advisors suggest portfolios according to market trends and risk tolerance.

- An AI assistant, for instance, examines market data and makes investing recommendations.

Personalized Financial Planning: AI chatbots help customers manage their debt, set savings objectives, and create budgets.

- For instance, based on spending patterns and income, a virtual assistant makes monthly savings recommendations.

Real-Time Market Insights: AI keeps an eye on financial markets and notifies users of noteworthy developments.

- As an illustration, a chatbot for the stock market alerts investors to changes in price and earnings updates.

Conversational AI increases convenience, strengthens security, and gives customers better tools for making financial decisions by automating financial services.

## 8.4 AI in Education: Tailored Instruction and Guidance

Conversational AI is changing education by increasing accessibility, personalization, and interaction. AI-powered virtual assistants and tutoring programs assist students in tracking their progress, understanding difficult ideas, and getting immediate feedback.

### Tutoring and Learning Support Driven by AI

Personalized Learning Paths: AI modifies lesson plans according to each student's learning preferences and progress.

- For instance, a virtual instructor can pinpoint a student's areas of weakness in mathematics and offer specific practice.

Instant schoolwork Assistance: AI assistants give students detailed explanations to aid them with their schoolwork.

- For instance, a chatbot uses interactive examples to clarify algebraic concepts.

Language Learning and Pronunciation Training: AI chatbots help with pronunciation correction and language practice.

- Example: A virtual language tutor delivers real-time feedback on speech and grammar.

**AI in Education and Management**

Automated Grading and Feedback: AI assesses homework and offers tailored comments.

- For instance, AI evaluates written writings for plagiarism, consistency, and language.

Gamified AI systems use challenges and quizzes to improve learning experiences, which in turn increases student motivation and engagement.

- Example: A chatbot rewards students with points for completing lectures and quizzes.

Accessibility for Students with Disabilities: AI-powered tools aid students with visual or hearing problems.

- For instance, a speech-to-text assistant records lectures for students who are hard of hearing.

Students gain from more efficient, personalized, and interesting learning experiences when AI is incorporated into the classroom, and teachers gain from less administrative work and more effective instruction.

Through increased accessibility, customisation, and efficiency, conversational AI is revolutionizing a number of industries. AI improves service quality and automates repetitive questions in e-commerce and customer support. Virtual assistants in the healthcare industry offer mental health support and medical advice. AI-powered banking and investment tools boost the finance industry, and AI-powered administrative support and individualized teaching are revolutionizing education.

AI will have increasingly complex uses as it develops, which will further change how people and organizations use technology. Organizations looking to enhance user experiences and streamline processes must comprehend and apply AI-driven conversational solutions.

# CHAPTER 9

## CONVERSATIONAL AI'S DIFFICULTIES AND RESTRICTIONS

In recent years, conversational AI has advanced remarkably, changing industries and improving user experiences in a variety of fields. But even with these developments, there are still many obstacles and restrictions that limit its capacity to accurately mimic human speech and intelligence. These obstacles include unresolved research questions that will influence the direction of AI development in the future, performance and scalability limitations, linguistic and cultural hurdles, and challenges in handling complicated discussions.

The basic constraints of conversational AI are examined in this chapter, along with the difficulties encountered in practical applications and the current research initiatives aimed at resolving them.

# 9.1 Comprehending and Managing Complicated Discussions

Chatbots and voice assistants are examples of conversational AI systems that frequently have trouble with complex, multi-turn interactions that call for long-term memory recall, logical reasoning, and contextual awareness. AI-based interactions are still heavily limited by their predetermined training data, algorithms, and computer resources, in contrast to human talks, which flow dynamically with numerous contextual references.

## Main Difficulties in Managing Complicated Discussions

### Context Retention and Memory Limitations

AI has trouble preserving context over prolonged exchanges.

- If a conversation goes on for more than a few turns, it frequently resets or loses coherence.
- For instance, because the system is unable to remember previous context, a consumer talking with a banking chatbot might have to repeat their account information several times during a session.

## Multi-Intent Recognition

- A single sentence in human discussions frequently has many intentions.
- AI models have trouble correctly recognizing and reacting to several intentions at once.
- An answer that only handles one request at a time might be given to a user who asks, "Can you check my account balance and transfer $500 to my savings?"

The use of ambiguous phrases, slang, or unfinished sentences by people necessitates contextual interpretation. This is known as "ambiguity and vagueness in human language."

- Because AI lacks profound comprehension, it may produce responses that are generic or unrelated.
- For instance, when someone asks, "Is it cold there?" In order to give a relevant response, AI might not accurately infer the user's position and context.

## Managing Topic Switching and Interruptions

Topic changes occur often throughout conversations,

therefore the AI must handle these changes fluidly.

- AI assistants usually struggle to deal with disruptions or sudden shifts in the topic of conversation.
- An AI system might become confused, for instance, if a consumer switches from talking about a problem with their order to asking about a refund policy.

Advanced neural network designs, reinforcement learning models, and hybrid AI strategies that blend deep learning and symbolic reasoning are being used in the fight to overcome these obstacles. But before conversational AI can match human-level discourse capabilities, a lot more work needs to be done.

## 9.2 Breaking Through Cultural and Linguistic Barriers

Regional dialects, cultural quirks, and contextual differences all impact how individuals interact, making language intrinsically complicated. Understanding and producing linguistically and culturally accurate responses are major challenges for conversational AI systems, especially those intended for worldwide deployment.

# Important Linguistic and Cultural Adaptation Challenges

Regional dialects and colloquialisms are difficult for AI models trained on standard language datasets to understand.

- For instance, a chatbot educated on American English might not be able to comprehend all of the idioms used in Scottish or Nigerian English.

## Multilingual Conversations and Code-Switching

- Many speakers transition between languages (code-switching) throughout the same conversation.
- Generally speaking, AI systems are unable to switch between languages with ease.
- For instance, if a user is bilingual in Spanish and English and says, "I need ayuda with my bank account," an AI system that isn't trained for mixed-language input may become confused.

## Ethical Considerations and Cultural Sensitivities

AI needs to be sensitive to cultural differences in order to prevent improper or offensive reactions.

- Word selections, degrees of formality, and politeness tactics are all influenced by cultural standards.

- For instance, direct communication is more typical in Western cultures, yet formal honorifics (such as "san") are expected in Japanese interactions.

Bias in Language Models: AI models produce stereotypes or mistakes as a result of inheriting biases from training data.

- In AI-generated content, bias might take the form of regional differences, gender, or ethnicity.

- For instance, it has long been discovered that AI voice assistants struggle with South Asian or African accents but excel with American or British ones.

Diversifying training data, involving language specialists in model construction, and incorporating real-time learning processes to adjust to a variety of linguistic and cultural inputs are all necessary steps for AI developers to overcome these problems.

## 9.3 Problems with Scalability and Performance

Conversational AI needs to be able to handle big user bases without sacrificing response quality, maintain high performance under a range of loads, and guarantee low latency in order to be successfully implemented at scale. However, there are a number of obstacles in the way of reaching this degree of scalability.

### Primary Issues with Scalability and Performance

### Latency and Response Time

- In order to process queries and produce real-time responses, AI models need a significant amount of processing power.
- Response time delays, particularly in voice-based interactions, can have a detrimental effect on the user experience.
- For instance, people used to quick responses may become irritated if a customer support chatbot takes a few seconds to answer.

### Computational expenses and Resource Limitations

- High operating expenses result from the substantial infrastructure needed to run large-scale AI models.
- Cloud-based AI systems must strike a balance between cost and performance.
- For instance, server and maintenance costs may make it too expensive for an organization to implement conversational AI on-premises.

## Scalability in High-Traffic Scenarios

- AI systems need to be able to handle large volumes of traffic without experiencing performance degradation.
- Example: During flight cancellations, an airline chatbot may see a spike in inquiries, necessitating strong scalability measures.

## Data Storage and Privacy Concerns

- AI systems store enormous volumes of data on user interactions, which raises security and privacy issues.
- Adherence to data regulations such as the CCPA and GDPR is crucial.
- For instance, in order to adhere to privacy

regulations, a healthcare chatbot must guarantee that patient data is handled safely.

Optimizing AI models, utilizing cloud computing, utilizing edge AI for localized processing, and putting effective caching techniques into place to improve reaction times are all necessary to meet these problems.

## 9.4 Upcoming Problems and Research Topics

Even though conversational AI is still developing, there are still a number of significant obstacles that will influence its future. To create AI interactions that are more ethical, contextually aware, and human-like, researchers and practitioners of AI must overcome these challenges.

### Primary Upcoming Obstacles

### True Natural Language Understanding (NLU)

- AI still has trouble understanding comedy, idioms, sarcasm, and deeper comprehension.
- For instance, an AI system might take the inquiry "Can you pass the salt?" literally instead of

understanding it as a courteous request.

## Emotional Intelligence and Empathy

- AI is unable to "feel" emotions, which makes it difficult to respond with empathy.
- An example would be if I responded to a user who was grieving by using general terms instead of sensitive, tailored ones.

## Unsupervised Learning and Self-Improvement

- Labeled datasets are a major component of current models, and unsupervised learning is still a major area of research interest.
- Artificial intelligence (AI) systems of the future must be able to learn from real-world encounters without requiring a lot of human intervention.

## Ethical AI Development and Bias Mitigation

- Ensuring fairness in AI models is still a difficulty.
- For instance, while assessing applicants, AI recruitment systems must steer clear of racial and gender biases.

**Integration with Augmented and Virtual Reality (AR/VR)**

- Although integration is still difficult, conversational AI will be essential to immersive experiences.
- For instance, in order to improve user interaction, AI-driven virtual assistants in metaverse contexts require sophisticated conversational skills.

Developments in deep learning, reinforcement learning, and neuro-symbolic AI are critical to the development of conversational AI. In order to make AI more responsive, context-aware, and able to engage in natural human contact, these issues must be resolved.

Although conversational AI has advanced significantly, there are still many obstacles to overcome. Research is still being done on handling complex interactions, overcoming linguistic and cultural obstacles, guaranteeing performance scalability, and addressing potential AI limitations. Even if conversational agents driven by AI are becoming better, real human-like intelligence and interaction are still a ways off.

Future AI research will concentrate on overcoming these constraints in order to create more sophisticated, ethical, and context-aware AI systems that have the potential to revolutionize how people use technology.

# CHAPTER 10

## CONVERSATIONAL AI'S FUTURE

Conversational AI is developing quickly and influencing how people use technology. Conversational systems are growing increasingly complex, perceptive, and human-like as a result of developments in deep learning, generative AI, and neural networks. But this development also brings up significant issues regarding the direction AI-powered communication may take in the future.

The pursuit of Artificial General Intelligence (AGI), the integration of conversational AI with IoT and smart devices, the importance of generative AI in developing conversational systems, and the major advancements influencing the future generation of AI-driven interactions are all covered in this chapter.

## 10.1 Generative AI's Function in Conversational Systems

Conversational AI has been transformed by generative AI, which allows computers to generate responses that are more coherent, creative, and contextually aware than those of a person. Generative AI models use deep learning techniques, especially large language models (LLMs), to create text dynamically based on input data, in contrast to typical rule-based chatbots that rely on prepared responses.

## Significant Progress in Conversational Systems Using Generative AI

### Contextual Awareness and Coherence

Generative AI models, like Google's Gemini and OpenAI's GPT series, evaluate enormous volumes of text data using transformer-based architectures to provide replies that preserve contextual consistency. Modern LLMs can track multi-turn interactions and modify responses appropriately, unlike previous models that had trouble with lengthy chats.

### Adaptive Learning and Personalization

- Generative AI learns from user preferences and behaviors to provide individualized user interactions.
- By customizing responses according on previous exchanges, AI assistants can increase user engagement and pleasure.

Instead of depending on pre-written responses, generative models can produce original, complex, and varied responses. This leads to Improved Language Understanding and Creativity.

- These systems are appropriate for a range of applications, such as customer service, education, and entertainment, because they can adjust to varied communication styles.

**Difficulties and Ethical Issues**

- Despite these developments, bias, false information, and hallucinations fabricated answers that seem real but aren't are issues with generative AI.
- It is still very difficult to guarantee that AI-generated material complies with ethical standards and factual accuracy.

The development of conversational AI will continue to heavily rely on generative AI, but its responsible use will depend on how bias, security, and dependability issues are resolved.

## 10.2 Conversational AI's Integration with Smart Devices and the Internet of Things

Conversational AI's capabilities have been extended by the Internet of Things (IoT), allowing voice-assisted interactions with wearables, industrial systems, smart home appliances, and driverless cars. The way individuals use technology in their daily lives is being completely transformed by this integration.

### How IoT and Smart Devices Are Improved by Conversational AI

### Smart Homes Activated by Voice
- Using natural language instructions, users may operate smart devices with AI-powered voice assistants like Apple Siri, Google Assistant, and Amazon Alexa.

- Users may control security systems, lighting, and temperature without using their hands.

## Seamless Integration in Automotive Systems

- By integrating with car infotainment systems, conversational AI is revolutionizing driving by providing hands-free communication, voice-based navigation, and real-time traffic updates.
- AI-powered assistants are also capable of detecting driver weariness and offering emergency support.

## Healthcare and Wearable Technology

- Conversational AI is used by wearable technology with AI integration, including fitness trackers and smartwatches, to provide real-time health information, reminders, and diagnostics.
- These technologies let users monitor vital signs, manage chronic disorders, and potentially identify early indicators of illnesses.

## IoT-AI Integration Challenges

- Privacy and Data Security: As smart devices gather enormous volumes of user data, worries about data privacy, security lapses, and illegal spying are raised.

- Latency and Connectivity Issues: High-speed connectivity is necessary for real-time AI processing, and user experience may be impacted by latency in cloud-based AI interactions.

- Standardization and Compatibility: It is difficult for devices from different manufacturers to work together because there are no common AI-IoT communication protocols.

More autonomous and intelligent settings are anticipated as conversational AI and IoT integration grows. But maintaining safe, dependable, and morally sound AI-IoT interactions continues to be of utmost importance.

## 10.3 Artificial General Intelligence (AGI) Journey

The creation of AI systems that can comprehend, learn, and carry out any intellectual work that a human can is known as artificial general intelligence, or AGI. AGI seeks to demonstrate reasoning, problem-solving, and adaptive learning across several domains, in contrast to narrow AI, which is made for specialized tasks.

## AGI Development to Date

### Deep Learning and Neural Network Advancements

- With the increasing sophistication of large-scale neural networks, AI models can now process and synthesize enormous volumes of data from many different fields.
- But in order to reach genuine generalization, AGI necessitates a fundamental change in AI architecture, not only deep learning.

Multimodal Artificial Intelligence Systems One important step toward AGI is the integration of speech, visual, text, and sensory input.

- AGI development requires AI models that can switch across modalities with ease (e.g., comprehending spoken instructions, identifying visual features, and performing actions).

### Reinforcement Learning and Self-Improvement

- AGI needs to learn on its own, gaining information without the aid of previously collected training data.

- A key element of this development is the use of reinforcement learning techniques, in which AI learns by making mistakes.

## Challenges and Ethical Considerations

- Computational Limitations: Large-scale implementation is challenging due to the enormous processing power and energy resources needed to achieve AGI.

- The development of artificial general intelligence (AGI) presents ethical issues pertaining to decision-making, control, and possible dangers in the event that AI outsmarts humans.

- Regulatory and Governance Issues: Institutions and governments need to set up procedures to guarantee that AGI is created in a way that is safe and does not endanger society.

Although artificial general intelligence (AGI) is still a theoretical goal, advances in neural networks, reinforcement learning, and self-improving AI models indicate that the field is moving in the right direction.

## 10.4 Conversational AI: What's Next?

With developments that will improve user interactions, broaden AI's potential, and rethink human-AI cooperation, conversational AI is set for major breakthroughs in the future.

## New Developments and Trends

## Highly customized AI assistants

- AI will provide highly customized conversational experiences based on user choices, emotional states, and behavioral patterns, going beyond generic interactions.

- Emotionally Intelligent AI: Affective computing will be included into future AI models, enabling them to recognize and react to human emotions with more emotional intelligence and empathy.

- Decentralized AI and Edge Computing: By processing data locally on devices instead of transferring it to centralized servers, AI models will move from cloud-based systems to edge computing, improving privacy and lowering latency.

- Contextual and Multimodal AI: Multimodal capabilities will be included into future AI systems, allowing them to comprehend and react to inputs in the form of text, audio, images, and video with ease.

- Regulatory and Ethical AI Governance: To guarantee openness, responsibility, and moral AI application, governments and regulatory organizations will set up extensive AI governance frameworks.

A future where human-computer interactions are more organic, intuitive, and advantageous is being shaped by the development of conversational AI. However, understanding the long-term effects of conversational AI on society will require addressing security issues, assuring ethical AI research, and bringing AI innovations into line with human values.

Conversational AI has already revolutionized human-machine interaction, and it has even more promise for the future. The next phase of AI-powered communication will be characterized by the development of generative AI, IoT integration, AGI advancement, and personalized and emotionally intelligent AI.

AI will become more human-like in its comprehension and reactivity as research advances, improving accessibility, ease, and productivity across industries. However, in order to guarantee a future in which AI benefits and serves humanity responsibly, the ethical, security, and governance issues related to AI must be properly addressed.

# ABOUT THE AUTHOR

 Author and thought leader in the IT field Taylor Royce is well known. He has a two-decade career and is an expert at tech trend analysis and forecasting, which enables a wide audience to understand complicated concepts.

Royce's considerable involvement in the IT industry stemmed from his passion with technology, which he developed during his computer science studies. He has extensive knowledge of the industry because of his experience in both software development and strategic consulting.

Known for his research and lucidity, he has written multiple best-selling books and contributed to esteemed tech periodicals. Translations of Royce's books throughout the world demonstrate his impact.

Royce is a well-known authority on emerging technologies and their effects on society, frequently requested as a speaker at international conferences and as a guest on tech podcasts. He promotes the development of ethical technology, emphasizing problems like data privacy and the digital divide.

In addition, with a focus on sustainable industry growth, Royce mentors upcoming tech experts and supports IT education projects. Taylor Royce is well known for his ability to combine analytical thinking with technical know-how. He sees a time when technology will ethically benefit humanity.